THE WEE TREASURY OF ALTERNATIVE SWEAR OPTIONS FOR NEW PARENTS

THE WEE TREASURY OF ALTERNATIVE SWEAR OPTIONS FOR NEW PARENTS

...and for Those Who Want to Keep it Mild

MARSTON LYONS

Marston Lyons

CONTENTS

Dedication vi

1 A Collection of Alternative Swears...Easy as ABC   3

2 Suggested Alternative Swears by Emotion ...Finding Just the Right Words for Any Occasion   12

3 Alternative Swears That Are Rhetorical Questions ...But Do They Really Need Answers?   17

4 Build a Swear Workshop ....Create Your Own or Find a New Favorite!   19

5 Famous People Mentioned in Alternative Swears ...Because They Are Rad Glass Mother Butters!   22

6 Famous Quotes ...But Don't Quote Us!   24

7 Even More Famous Quotes ...No Subtitle Needed Here!   25

8 Mild Closing Thoughts ...From Here to Eternity   26

Dedicated to The Three Wise Guys

Copyright © 2021 by Marston Lyons

All rights reserved. No part of this book may be reproduced in any manner whatsoever without written permission except in the case of brief quotations embodied in critical articles and reviews.

ISBN-13: 978-1-7378044-2-0

First Printing, 2021

Cover design by: Marston Lyons

Introduction

Swearing is a way of life for many of us. It adds much needed pepper and excitement to our everyday boring vernacular. And most certainly, it is a much welcomed stress reliever. Swearing is a socially acceptable* (*to those who swear) way of blowing off steam that lets others within earshot know you've had enough of whatever it is you are swearing about.

Once we become parents, however, we realize that swearing like a sailor is perceived as wrong by many other people* (* people who don't swear). You realize that little impressionable ears are listening to our every peppery word. You couldn't imagine if your child's first word was %$#@! What would the neighbors say?

Yes, you've reached a point in your life as a new parent where you need to take a verbal step back. You need to make venting steam a mild expression of not being able to take one more minute of whatever it is you want to swear about. You now realize you are crossing the threshold of mild verbal venting by way of "parentally approved alternative swearing." What is this, you may ask? You are probably familiar with these mild expressive sayings from your own youth. Perhaps when your babysitter would say out loud "SUGAR HONEY ICED TEA!" - when at the time you thought she was just preparing your lunch. With a new and impressionable baby in the home, you see the clouds have parted and the sky is wide open to the endless possibilities of alternative swearing. Verbally venting to release steam or amazement, but gentle enough to be said in the vicinity of a church.

But how the %$#! can this be done, you may ask? Easy. A swear does not need to be a swear. There are expressions called euphemisms that are just similar ways to say things, but cleverly altered so they are not offensive to the gentle ear. There is even an actual phrase called "minced oaths" which is how these non offensive euphemisms are categorized. As long as profanity has been around, there has been an equally opposing force trying to make things more pleasant to hear.

In writing this book, I have done the hard work for you. I went through all the archives of time and history that I could find and handpicked the most time-honored mild swears that mankind has achieved so far. I have assembled these expressions into this humble book and present them concisely to you. The following book is a collection of delightfully mild swears and exhalations that any parent may use as they see fit. For the more advanced alternative swearer, you can read on to our special "Build a Swear Workshop" chapter to mix and match a mildly gentle expression of grief or joy, of your very own. There's nothing like that feeling you get when you know your listening audience is wondering what lively expression of exasperation you may use next!

And now, without further ado... because I can feel the stress level climbing in the readership.... here are the top swear alternatives for new parents.... and anyone else who wants to keep it mild with clean verbal relief!

CHAPTER 1

A Collection of Alternative Swears...Easy as ABC

Following is an alphabetical listing of minced oaths, euphemisms, or whatever else you'd like to call alternative swears at this point. Sadly, not every letter has a swear "lite" to call it's own. If any readers out there can let me know of kinder swears for the following letters, I'd be happy to learn them! Letters missing from "The Wee Treasury of Alternative Swear Options for New Parents" are "K" "N" "Q" "U" "V" "X" and letters needing more swear alternatives are "A" "I" "P" "T." I included them in the list below so in case you find any you can pencil them in yourself!

A
Aww, Gee

B
Bejeebers
Begorrah
Blimey
By gum
By George
By cracky

C
Cheese and rice
Cheese and crackers
Crud
Cripe on a crud
Cripes
Criminy
Consarn it

D
Dadgummit
Dagnabbit
Dang it
Dang it all
Darn

Darn it all
Darn it to heck
Doggone
Doggonit
Drat

E
Egad
Egads
Eureka

F
Fiddlesticks
Fiddly Diddly
Fe Fi Fiddly Diddly
Fiddly Fudge
Fork it
For crying out loud
For fudge sakes
For Pete's sake
For cripes sake
For the love of the lard
Fink
Frig
Frig it
Flipping
For goodness sakes

Frickin
Frizzle frazzle
Fricking
Fudge
Fudge it
Fudge it all
Futz

G
Gah
Gee whillikers
Glass
Gobsmacked
Good gravy
Good golly
Good golly Miss Molly
Good lard
Good lardy
Gosh
Gee
Geeze
Great Caesar's ghost
Great Scott
Gadzooks
Goodness me
Goodness sakes
Good gracious
Goodness gracious me oh my
Good grief

Good gravy
Gosh darned
Gosh dang it
Gosh darn it

H
Heavens to Betsy
Heavens to murgatroyds
Heck
Heck no
H-E - double hockey sticks
Hells bells
Holy moly
Holy smit
Holy schnikes

I
I don't give a darn
I don't give a gosh darn

J
Jeepers
Jeepers creepers
Jumping jiminy
Jiminy crickets
Judas priest

Jason crisp
Jinkys
Jeebus
Jeepers creepers
Jumping Jehoshaphat
Jumping Jupiter

K

L
Land sakes
Lard have mercy
Lardy
Lardy me

M
Mercy me
My gosh
My word
My stars
Mother butter

N

O
Oh for goodness sakes
Oh my stars
Oh my goodness
Oh my heck
Oh mylanta
Oh dear
Oh dear bread and beer

P
Pain in the glass

Q

R
Rats
Ratfink

S
Sakes alive
Smit
Shut the front door
Son of a gun
Son of a pup
Son of a switch
Son of a switch on a stitch

Sufferin succotash
Sugar honey iced tea

T
Tarnation

U

V

W
Well I'll be
Well I'll be darned
What in tarnation
What the bejeebers
What the smit
What the hay
What the heck
Where the frig
Why the fudge
What in the world
What in the name of all that is holy
What in Sam Hill
What the fudge
Who the hay
When the fork
What the futz

Well I never
What in the world
What in the world is that
What in the world is going on

X

Y
Yippee kai yay mother butters

Z
Zounds

CHAPTER 2

Suggested Alternative Swears by Emotion ...Finding Just the Right Words for Any Occasion

Learning when and where to say what will be easier once you get the gist with the following list. I have listed a few emotional triggers for peppery language and offered a few suggested alternative expressions. This is just to get you thinking along the lines of turning sharp barbs into a fluff of cotton candy.

So where are your alternative swears needed at this time? Follow our "Emotional Swear Alternative Translator" below to pinpoint the most accurate mild verbal expression you need right now.

EMOTIONAL SWEAR ALTERNATIVE TRANSLATOR

Anger:
Son of a switch on a stitch
Dagnabbit

Fear:
Goodness gracious me oh my
Cripes

Joy:
Cheese and rice
Gee whillikers

Exasperation:
For the love of the lard
Consarn it

Euphoria:
Yippee kai yay mother butters
Eureka

Hunger:
For fudge sakes
Fork it

Boredom:
Egads
Good grief

Contempt:
Fe fi fiddly diddly
Begorrah

Exhaustion:
Drat
Good lard

Gassy:
Cheese and crackers
Frizzle Frazzle

Bewildered:
Blimey
Gadzooks

Indifference:
Geez
Gah

Frustrated:
Fiddlesticks
Dadgummit

Inquisitive:
Great Caesar's Ghost
What in the name of the world

Contrary:
What in tarnation
Ratfink

Sassy:
Sugar honey iced tea
Jumping Jehoshaphat

CHAPTER 3

Alternative Swears That Are Rhetorical Questions ...But Do They Really Need Answers?

What the golly?

How the futz?

When in the world?

Where in tarnation?

Why in Sam Hill?

Where the jingle bells?

Why the hay?

What the bejeebers?

How the jumping Jehosaphat?

Who the fork?

How the cripes?

Who the what the?

When the smit?

Why the switch?

Where the schnikes?

CHAPTER 4

Build a Swear Workshop ....Create Your Own or Find a New Favorite!

Now that you have studied up on the many types of mild alternative swears that are out there, you are ready to move on to our advanced class. So put on your artist's smock and let's get creative!

Using the following two step process below, you are free to invent an alternative swear expression to call your very own. It's as easy as can be! Simply take an interesting word from the Build a Swear Workshop "Word Bank" found below. Use this word to fill in the blank on the "Euphemistic Expression Maker" listed below it. Mix and match as you please!

BUILD A SWEAR WORKSHOP

WORD BANK

PUP
GUM
SWITCH
FRIG
GOLLY
SMIT
GRAVY
CRIPES
HAY
FUDGE
LARD
JINGLE BELLS
SAM HILL
DARN
FORK
HECK
FUTZ
CRISP
BEJEEBERS

EUPHEMISTIC EXPRESSION MAKER

What the_____
Son of a_____
Who the_____
What in the_____
When the_____
Where the_____
How in the_____
Why in the_____
For the love of a_____
For crying out_____
Oh my_____

You may notice that some of these make an incomplete statement. But who really needs a complete thought once you've vented your peppery phrase? Your work here is done.

CHAPTER 5

Famous People Mentioned in Alternative Swears ...Because They Are Rad Glass Mother Butters!

Sam Hill

Judas Priest

Jehoshaphat

Miss Molly

Jiminy Crickets

THE WEE TREASURY OF ALTERNATIVE SWEAR OPTIONS FOR NEW PARENTS - 23

Caesar

Scott

Pete

Betsy

Jason Crisp

CHAPTER 6

Famous Quotes ...But Don't Quote Us!

"@#%$% *&^$$"
    -You, earlier this year

"^(&%((!%^$"
    -That person at that place that one time

"&(*)&*T% $*&^"
    - Overheard in public somewhere

")(&)(*%@#$^"
    - That person waiting in line at that store

CHAPTER 7

Even More Famous Quotes ...No Subtitle Needed Here!

"I've been accused of vulgarity. I'd say that's bullshit."
-Mel Brooks

"'Twas but my tongue, 'twas not my soul that swore"
- Euripides

"When a gentleman is disposed to swear, it is not for any standers-by to curtail his oaths."
-William Shakespeare

CHAPTER 8

Mild Closing Thoughts ...From Here to Eternity

So there you have it. You now have at your fingertips a complete treasure trove of gentle expressions that you can utter guilt free to your heart's content. Feel free to use these sayings as you see fit for every stop on your emotional rainbow.

Mildly yours,
Marston Lyons

www.ingramcontent.com/pod-product-compliance
Lightning Source LLC
Chambersburg PA
CBHW072210100526
44589CB00015B/2465